31 Days of Confidence
Engage Your Core and Leadership

By: Christin L. Webb

Copyright © 2024 Christin L. Webb
All rights reserved.
ISBN-979-8-9896008-0-9
The Greater You Leadership Series

Front cover and inside photography by @ 2023 Talisha Ingram. All rights reserved.

This book is a work of fiction and non-fiction. Names, characters, places, and incidents either are the author's personal experience, imagination, or are used fictitiously. Any resemblance to actual persons, living or dead, events, locales, or organization is entirely coincidental.

All rights reserved. No part of this document may be reproduced or transmitted in any form or by any means, electronic, mechanical, photocopying, recording, or otherwise, without prior written permission of Christin Webb.

To every person who has ever experienced self-doubt or disbelief in themselves. There is a point of return. Let us find it together.

This book is dedicated to my mother, Sylvia Webb. She inspires me in ways she may never know. I am who I am because of who she is.

Table of Contents

From The Author 9
How To Use This Book 11
What Is Confidence? 14
What Is Leadership? 16
What Is Shared Confidence? 17
The Confidence Strategy 19
Confidence Pre-Assessment 21
Week 1: Understand You 24
    EVERY PIECE OF YOU 25
    STEP 1: UNDERSTAND YOU 28
Week 2: Capitalize On You 37
    IT IS ALREADY THERE 38
    STEP 2: CAPITALIZE ON YOU 40
Week 3: Identify Confidence Barriers 49
    THE SQUARE CIRCLE 50
    STEP 3: IDENTIFY CONFIDENCE BARRIERS 52
Week 4: Counteract Confidence Barriers 64
    THE OWL 65
    STEP 4: COUNTERACT CONFIDENCE BARRIERS 67
    CONFIDENCE BARRIER COUNTERACTIVE STRATEGY 69
Week 5: Inspire Confidence 77
    THE LEGACY OF WOMEN'S MONTH 78
    STEP 5: INSPIRE CONFIDENCE 80
    B.U.I.L.D. SHARED CONFIDENCE 82
Confidence Post-Assessment 88
Confidence Goals 91
Appendix 93
Confidence Assessment Scorecard 94
About The Author 99

From the Author

I have learned, the most effective leaders have a clear understanding of who they are as individuals before, during, and after they lead. That understanding is fostered by the level of self-awareness and confidence possessed  and executed in any given situation. As we grow, the goal for many is to become more in tune with self. It is that internal connectivity that drives our skills and abilities, and our style of leadership and its potential in creating success for everyone influenced by our leadership.

Every successful personal and professional experience or relationship I have had in the last 20+ years directly correlated with the level of confidence I embraced and executed. Therefore, one of my foundational ideologies is to strengthen self-confidence to strengthen leadership. Doing so allows the core of an individual to ripple throughout every action, decision, relationship, and space we create. **31 Days of Confidence: Engage Your Core and Leadership** is an elevated level, transformative roadmap to self-discovery that offers strategic and key concepts to help develop and manage individual and shared confidence while integrating it into leading self and others.

I realize that supporting confidence and leadership includes identifying resources. I wanted to create a resource; a tool that allowed for reflection and creativity, not just a feel-good book. So, while there are thoughtful motivational components within the book including daily affirmations or short stories of confidence in action this is an interactive guide of tools. Utilizing the tools in this resource, individuals will be empowered to navigate leadership with more authenticity; boldly and strategically.

"You cannot stumble upon greatness; you walk up to it and introduce yourself."
Christin L Webb

How to Use This Book

This interactive book compiles diverse educational and inspirational strategies aimed at boosting self-confidence, leadership skills, and mutual assurance. It offers a roadmap for cultivating and sustaining self-confidence, emphasizing that the effort invested yields corresponding results.

Book Effectiveness

This book is designed as a 31-day program. If used in a month that does not have 31 days, continue the program into the beginning of the next month. To fully benefit from the Confidence Strategy™, it is important to follow the book in the order it is presented, as it is structured for incremental learning and development.

Confidence Strategy

The book is based on The Greater You Leadership Series' Confidence Strategy, encompassing five steps. These steps guide individuals in developing self-awareness, accountability, communication, and servant leadership, all integral to building confidence. Each week focuses on one of these steps, complemented by specific lessons and activities to reinforce the concepts, ensuring a comprehensive and practical approach to enhancing confidence.

Confidence Assessments

At the start and end of this journey, Confidence Assessments are offered to pinpoint the current level of self-confidence. This aids in identifying which areas need attention to reduce or eliminate obstacles to achieving high confidence. The supplementary tools included in this guide are designed to enhance the results of these assessments.

Motivational Affirmations and Prompts

The book offers a series of 31 daily motivational affirmations and prompts, aligning with the Confidence Strategy. These affirmations are designed to be adaptable to individual needs and preferences. They can be engaged in several ways, such as reading aloud, writing, meditating, or even dancing to them, allowing for a personalized approach to enhancing confidence.

Daily Confidence Reflection

Daily, the book provides a chance to reflect on the motivational affirmations and prompts and assess how they relate to one's confidence levels that day. This reflection is an opportunity to pinpoint areas of improvement and strategize ways to bolster confidence for the following day.

Stories of Confidence

In the book, a mix of short fictional and non-fictional stories, drawing from real-life experiences, are woven throughout to illustrate the role and significance of confidence in both personal and professional contexts. These stories serve to highlight practical examples and the real-world impact of confidence.

31 Days of Confidence
Engage Your Core and Leadership

What Is Confidence?

It is important to know what confidence is to achieve goals or help others achieve them. It is simple yet complex in the same breath. It includes layers and layers of characteristics that help shape how it shows up for everyone. Here are just a few considerations for understanding confidence and its importance for managing it.

<u>Self-Assurance</u>: Confidence is a feeling of deep self-assurance arising from appreciation of one's existence, abilities, skills, gifts, talents, or qualities. Confidence is knowing the value one offers in any situation and displaying it in a way that clearly conveys it to others. It is believing in self. Having confidence does not rid internal or external challenges but allows an individual to draw from a space of self-assurance that pushes them to work through and beyond challenges.

<u>Hills & Valleys</u>: Confidence consists of hills and valleys. Varying circumstances, environments, and/or situations may drive the level of confidence an individual possesses. For example, just because a person is comfortable networking during a social event does not mean they possess the same level of confidence when required to speak in front of a crowd of hundreds. Further, our lives experience ebbs and flows in the way we are equipped to manage our confidence. An individual must be prepared to always anticipate the need to refresh their level of confidence. It is a cycle and should be treated accordingly.

<u>Multi-dimensional</u>: Confidence is dynamic and complex. It is multi-dimensional. It is layered with mental, emotional, and physical attributes. It begins internally and not externally. No article of clothing, job, relationship, or any other modern-day armor can create confidence. It comes from within a person and can only exist based on the intentional choice to trust and believe in self. The external

perception of confidence in others, or lack thereof, is a byproduct of the confidence that begins within a person.

Because confidence is multi-dimensional, it can be complex, and that fact should always be considered. We cannot expect to respond the same way every day for every situation. There are many factors that drive confidence and being self-aware and agile in managing self-confidence is the game changer.

What is Leadership?

Leadership is the ability to influence, direct, and guide people to move towards a common goal. It involves setting a clear vision, providing inspiration, and guiding others towards the attainment of shared objectives. Effective leaders possess qualities like decisiveness, empathy, integrity, and the ability to communicate effectively. They motivate and empower individuals or groups, fostering a supportive environment that encourages inclusivity, collaboration, and innovation. Leadership is not just about authority; it also involves listening, learning, and adapting to changing circumstances. Effective leadership is rooted in the leader's self-awareness and their confidence in leading.

What does self-confidence look like in leadership?

Simple. The same. It does not change. It is just as critical to have high or managed confidence when activating leadership. Success or lack of success in leadership depends on the level of self-confidence.

Effectively managed self-confidence allows leaders to embrace difficult and challenging moments. Self-confidence supports proactivity that cultivates environments that support vision, innovation, and other critical leadership skills needed. The correlation between confidence and leadership can be demonstrated when leading others. Many individuals can sense when someone is confident and when they are not. A leader perceived to not be confident by those they influence will quickly lose momentum in effectively impacting the team and meeting goals. The necessary trust and buy-in from those influenced by the leader may be harder to gain when they know the leader is not confident.

Choosing to enhance individual confidence is a strategic approach to leading more effectively.

What is Shared Confidence?

Have you ever had someone walk into a room of people where the energy was high and someone with incredibly low energy walked in and the mood in the room changed accordingly? Even on the opposite, have you experienced or heard of an instance where the energy in the room may have been low and someone with an elevated energy walked into the room and people's energy shifted to a higher level?

Energy is real. Its transferability is worth acknowledging and managing it effectively. This is the same for confidence. Confidence can be free-flowing and fluid just as energy can be. Confidence can adapt and apply a sense of self-assurance to different challenges and environments, demonstrating that confidence, much like a skill.

The way a leader's confidence shows up transfers to those influenced by their leadership. A leader with low confidence may find those they lead displaying examples of low confidence. Their work performance may be impacted. The team dynamics may appear less than desirable. On the contrary, a leader with well-managed confidence will lead while displaying examples of high confidence. The team and the organization will respond accordingly. Collaboration may be high. Communication may resonate effectively, interdepartmentally. In either instance, the leader's level of confidence impacts success and sustainability. The leader's confidence helps to drive a team or a community's motivations, its confidence as a team. That transfer or shift of energy then becomes shared energy.

Shared confidence is utilizing individual confidence and fostering confidence that is shared among teams, organizations, and communities. Shared confidence supports long-term success and sustainability. It exists best when team dynamics have been established and cohesiveness exists. Successful shared confidence is evident where effective leadership is cultivated. Consider assessing your team or organization's shared confidence.

The Confidence Strategy

In life, thus in leadership, action without a defined plan can be a recipe for chaos and failure. Like any goal, outlining a strategy is critical. A strategy in its purest form provides a clear roadmap towards achieving specific goals or objectives.

A well-defined strategy helps in focusing efforts and resources efficiently, allows for proactive planning, and aids in anticipating potential challenges or opportunities. It creates a framework for decision-making, ensuring actions are aligned with the intended direction. Additionally, a strategy can improve coordination and communication within a team or organization, fostering a unified approach towards common aims. This focus and direction are essential for effectively managing resources, navigating complexities, and achieving desired outcomes.

Developing and managing your confidence should be executed using a strategy. Your strategy should be an intentional thought process wrapped in significant planned actions that align with the necessary tools and ideologies to secure your confidence in any situation.

This book offers a five-step strategy that outlines reflective moments to become more self-aware and define activities to help increase high confidence on an individual level and identify ways to help inspire confidence in others; specifically, those you lead.

In the subsequent pages, you will be able to create a confidence strategy customized to your needs and based upon your transparent and honest reflections using the following steps:

Step 1: Understand You
Step 2: Capitalize on You
Step 3: Identify Confidence Barriers

Step 4: Counteract Confidence Barriers
Step 5: Inspire Confidence

By the end of step 5, you will have created a personalized roadmap for your individual and shared confidence.

It should be noted that the uniqueness of using the confidence strategy is that it can be used repeatedly. Just like the wind, we change. With that change requires continued exploration of self, thus our confidence. Revisit the confidence strategy regularly to identify areas that may need new, more, or less attention to manage self-confidence.

As much as we may want, we never remain the same.

Confidence Pre-Assessment
Rate Your Existing Level of Confidence

The Confidence Assessment is a dynamic tool designed to measure your confidence at various stages of your life. Answer each question below and put an 'X' according to the column that is more responsive to the corresponding question. The scorecard is available in the Appendix to identify your results.

It is important to recognize that maintaining a specific confidence level is a deliberate decision. Thus, you should consciously and regularly engage in self-assessment. Make sure to use this tool at regular intervals.

Questions	Not At All	Rarely	Sometimes	Often	Very Often
In my actions, I often prioritize societal expectations over my personal convictions of what's truly right.					
Navigating new scenarios, I find myself adapting with a sense of ease and confidence.					
My outlook on life is generally upbeat and full of energy.					
Confronted with challenges that seem daunting, I'm inclined to step back rather than engage.					
Persistence is a trait I hold dear, continuing the effort where others might retreat.					
I'm convinced that diligence in problem-					

solving inevitably leads to uncovering solutions.					
Setting goals for myself, I consistently meet them.					
Encountering difficulties can sometimes leave me feeling defeated and pessimistic.					
I empathize with those who invest immense effort yet find their goals just out of reach.					
The feedback I receive on my endeavors and accomplishments is often affirmative.					
Without early signs of success in my endeavors, my motivation tends to wane.					
When I overcome a challenge, I reflect on the insights gained from the experience.					
I hold a firm belief that dedication and hard work pave the way to achieving my aspirations.					
My circle includes individuals whose skills and achievements I admire and deem successful.					

Source: Adapted from MindTools.com and retrieved from the resource article: How Self-Confident Are You? Improving Self-Confidence by Building Self-Efficacy

TOTAL SCORE: _____

	Score Interpretations
14-32	You might be yearning for a boost in self-assurance! Consider reflecting on your accomplishments. Often, it's easy to dwell on what's missing, overshadowing the appreciation and application of your unique skills and talents.
33-51	You're somewhat on track with acknowledging your capabilities and trusting in what you can do. However, you might be setting the bar too high for yourself, which can hinder you from fully embracing and benefiting from your expertise.
52-70	Outstanding! You excel at extracting lessons from each experience and you don't let challenges diminish your self-view. Remember, there's always space for personal growth. Continue to cultivate your self-confidence with care.

The most sustainable path to success is to engage your core...

Week 1: Understand You

"You cannot stumble upon greatness; you walk up to it and introduce yourself."
Christin L Webb

Every Piece of You

Since I was seven years old, I knew I wanted to be a 'boss.' At least that is what I called anyone I saw as a leader. Whether I was watching the primetime show on television or attending church, I was always able to identify the person I observed as having the most influence in the space they were in. I understood early on that influence meant getting things done. I equated influence to being able to sustain a lifestyle that a person wanted. From my seven-year-old view, influence carried a briefcase, wore chic, bold, and commanding suits, and walked with a stride of confidence with every foot met to the ground. I perceived influence to begin in the boardrooms or important meeting halls and impacted individuals and communities. I wanted to be a leader.

Influenced by my dad's love and skill for writing, I began authoring poems and short plays at an early age. My dad, the same person that influenced my love for using my imagination and creativity was the same person I watched simultaneously struggle and thrive with his passion for writing. His struggle stuck out to me the most. It was often tied to other uncomfortable moments in my life. And while I never fully let go of my creativity, I put more effort into getting into those boardrooms and meeting halls and often boxed my creativity out of my life. I have written plays, short films, novels, documentaries, corporate training scripts, and more. I have taken several stages to sing, dance, or act. Yet, I never truly embraced my creativity. Heck, if anyone has ever asked me what I do, I rarely part my lips and say a creative. It is always last on my list. I thought his lessons were mine, yet they were. Not lessons to deter me, but to educate me on how to best manage self.

My first corporate position was at 18 years old. I did what I felt to be 'practical' and earned my bachelor's and master's degrees. I was consistently promoted to positions that I only dreamt of as a seven-year-old little girl. I garnered solid networks locally and nationally and gained the respect from my associates and colleagues I often sought out. I was a mentee and mentor to many. I earned certifications, attended professional conferences, and volunteered for the organizations I worked for and others within the community, locally and nationally. A little over 20 years later, I finally reached the corner office with the perfect view of the city's skyline, a respectable salary, all to find out that my happiness was incomplete. I did everything 'right.' At least right for me at the time. My achievements, while I needed them and am grateful for the growth that came out of each, I knew I had reached my limit inside the box I had placed myself in when I was seven years old.

I spent forty years torn between my desire to lead or influence an organization, executing business acumen, while also living out my creativity. I believed I had to choose which piece of me I could show to the world. I chose the 'safe' route and while to others I appeared to excel, the lack of accountability and authenticity with myself, to myself, had become emotionally, mentally, and physically dangerous to my very being. I became ineffectively effective at compartmentalizing my world.

I realized I needed to do a different self-assessment on myself. I began asking what truly made me happy. What brought me joy? What made me complete? The answer. Every piece of who I was. There was not one specific piece of me that could be left on its own and create sustainability for me. I was able to answer that question. It moved me to begin assessing who I had been, was, and wanted to be. Even further, is it who I present as or truly am? Addressing each gave me a sense of clarity on my next steps. I have a greater sense of what drives me, motivates me, restricts me, propels me, and more. I liked some of the answers and others I learned they needed to be realigned or recalibrated. Behind all of it, my confidence grew even more (and it continues). I realized the choices I had been making impacted my overall confidence.

It is important for us to have the right level of self-awareness to truly navigate life; to navigate the things we want for our lives. We must be willing to explore the tough questions and seek out the answers until they are found. Whether we are supporting our loved ones and communities or simply starting new hobbies and passions, we owe it to ourselves to do it all while understanding ourselves during every new chapter. Had I not elected to have that moment of accountability with myself, who knows where I would be today. Who knows if even this piece of work would exist. I am glad we will never have to find out.

Understanding self is the real win.

Step 1: Understand You

Begin exploring and planning your strategy of confidence by understanding who you are as an individual as you understand yourself and not as others have told you. Do not explore you only in the present tense but explore who you have been in your past experiences and your expectations for yourself in the future.

Who have you been?

```
```

Who are you today?

```
```

Who are you becoming?

31 Days of Confidence: Engage Your Core and Leadership

Day 1

Yes, I can start today.

DAILY CONFIDENCE REFLECTION

Day 2

I am what I define.

DAILY CONFIDENCE REFLECTION

Day 3

I cannot skip the process and gain value.

DAILY CONFIDENCE REFLECTION

31 Days of Confidence: Engage Your Core and Leadership

Day 4

Realize me.

DAILY CONFIDENCE REFLECTION

Day 5

I do not share the responsibility for their faults.

DAILY CONFIDENCE REFLECTION

Day 6

My timing is defined for me.

DAILY CONFIDENCE REFLECTION

Day 7

I quit whispering about my greatness.

DAILY CONFIDENCE REFLECTION

Week 2: Capitalize on You

"You cannot stumble upon greatness; you walk up to it and introduce yourself."

Christin L Webb

It Is Already There

A while back I was visiting my favorite local restaurant. It is a place "where-everybody-knows-your-name." It is family friendly and has some of the most delectable dishes. I could go there every day. What has become one of my expectations when I visit is to meet someone new, exchange lighthearted or thoughtful conversations, even exchange information for later connections.

I recall a specific evening. I walked in and greeted my favorite server. She responded with delight, and I immediately saw many faces I knew and met from previous visits. One of the faces was of a woman who had recently transitioned careers. She called me over to catch up. We briefed each other about our most recent endeavors. She proceeded to introduce me and two women that were with her. One woman shared with me that she had applied for a position with a national firm that same day but was worried about one of the requirements. She was not sure she had experience in the specific area and felt it would knock her out of the running to be considered for the position. I began to ask her questions about her experience and specific tasks that she had completed in the past. It may have been a project or a meeting that allowed her to gain experience in the specific area she was concerned about. In less than five minutes, she uncovered a lot about her skills and abilities. After talking it through, she realized she had more than enough experience in the requirement, feeling more confident about completing the process. We discussed a few other strategic approaches to seeking out that position and other things and returned to our meals.

When I left the restaurant that evening, the conversation made me think about the times I talked myself out of an opportunity because I did not 'think' I was equipped or qualified. In those moments, I had not taken the time to assess what was really in my toolbelt of skills. It is easy to be so close to something that the answer becomes blurred. The apparent becomes disregarded and shadowed by the surface. It is in our willingness to step back and assess our skills, talents, and abilities that we truly know what we are capable of. We become less likely to shy away from opportunities or take the journeys even when doubt may lurk in the shadows. For her, she was contemplating not following through with continued communications with the company. For me, in the past, it may have been continuing to work on a project that was not in my toolbelt of skill. Time lost and opportunities missed.

Without the realization and acceptance of our skills, talents, and abilities, we limit the capacity to capitalize and maximize ourselves. We limit our leveraging power to success. Life is a game of chess and being able to understand your next move requires understanding what is in your toolbelt and how to use each tool effectively. If do not realize our skills, we do not realize our success. We then cannot create the plan and identify the resources required to get there.

Are you ready to capitalize on you?

Step 2: Capitalize On You

What are your skills, talents, and abilities? Your level of success depends on how you maximize each of them. By understanding more about yourself, you can identify ways to create even better versions of yourself and are further creating the path of your success.

What skills, talents, or abilities do you possess that you consider strong and helpful to your success?

What skills, talents, or abilities do you possess that you would like to enhance or that you would like to gain?

What are your achievements?

What would you like to achieve in the future?

Day 8

Walk in it.

DAILY CONFIDENCE REFLECTION

Day 9

I am willing to do the ordinary, unordinary, and extraordinary.

DAILY CONFIDENCE REFLECTION

Day 10

Boundaries support my sanity.

DAILY CONFIDENCE REFLECTION

Day 11

I live like I only get one shot.

DAILY CONFIDENCE REFLECTION

Day 12

I am unapologetically drawn to success.

DAILY CONFIDENCE REFLECTION

Day 13

My confidence impacts my excellence.

DAILY CONFIDENCE REFLECTION

Day 14

I was made for a time such as this.

DAILY CONFIDENCE REFLECTION

Week 3: Identify Confidence Barriers

"You cannot stumble upon greatness; you walk up to it and introduce yourself."

Christin L Webb

The Square Circle

I was in my early twenties and had been employed with the local utility company for close to 10 years. I was in my first year of college. Within those years, I was blessed to experience multiple promotions, always moving into roles that allowed me to explore more leadership and other beneficial business acumen. I was accustomed to applying for a position, being invited to an interview, and then being offered the position.

That was until I applied to become a Procurement Specialist in the Purchasing department. You are asking yourself, what is a Procurement Specialist? Heck, what is procurement? Do not worry. I asked myself that question when the position was posted to the job board. Back then, I had no clue, but I looked at that job board, saw the corresponding salary, and knew it was the job just for me.

Procurement buys. That is the quick answer. Now, the more thorough answer is that procurement is the inclusion of strategic methodologies utilized by professionals in organizations to procure or purchase goods and services needed to meet the business mission and goals. Back then, whatever it was, the Procurement Specialist was the job for me because it paid well and would support me and my young daughter financially.

I did what I always did when I was interested in an opportunity and submitted the application. A week or so went by and I was offered an interview. I remember walking into the interview with a hazy mind; not as clear. I sat in that interview chair across the table from two professionals; one was the Purchasing Supervisor, the other the Human Resources lead representative. They were polite and professional. They asked the questions and I assume words came out of my mouth because the interview eventually ended. I was nervous. I did not have answers that answered the questions asked. I demonstrated a lack of experience. What I also demonstrated was a lack of confidence. The lack of confidence was due to not doing the one thing I always did for an interview. What was that one thing you asked? Simple. I did not prepare.

When I am not prepared, I am not as confident as I need to be in those moments. It has shown up that way for me repeatedly. Many moments throughout my career when I was unprepared, my confidence was not either. That is the same others may experience as well. Preparation arms us with the knowledge, agility, flexibility, and awareness needed to navigate a moment successfully. Being unprepared and trying to be effective can be like trying to fit a square peg through a circle. It becomes the barrier to success; the barrier to confidently approaching situations.

What are your squared circles or barriers to confidence?

Step 3: Identify Confidence Barriers

There are multiple reasons for low confidence levels. Barriers, which can be individuals, groups, environments, or specific circumstances, function as obstacles preventing goal achievement. These barriers might not always be prominent in our lives. Recognizing what triggers confidence fluctuations and identifying potential barriers are crucial. This understanding enables the creation of effective strategies to overcome these obstacles and enhance confidence levels.

Below is a non-exhaustive list of potential barriers to high confidence. Mark each one that you have experienced being a limitation to demonstrating high confidence.

- Self-Defeating Assumptions   _____
- Goals that are too Big or Too Distant   _____
- Declaring Victory too Soon   _____
- Doing-it-yourself   _____
- Blaming Someone Else   _____
- Lack of Knowledge   _____
- Being Unprepared   _____
- Defensiveness   _____
- Entering Unknown Territory   _____
- Neglecting to Anticipate Setbacks   _____
- Rejection   _____
- Reflecting on Past Failures   _____
- Toxic people   _____
- Over-confidence   _____
- Conflict   _____
- Fear of Success   _____

Which barrier(s) can you relate to most? How did it make you feel when the barrier was experienced? Did you get past the barrier? If so, how? Are there other barriers you would include?

Day 15

Direct my energy in the positive.

DAILY CONFIDENCE REFLECTION

Day 16

I will make a decision and move on.

DAILY CONFIDENCE REFLECTION

Day 17

I realize who I am before someone else does.

DAILY CONFIDENCE REFLECTION

Day 18

There is beauty in vulnerability.

DAILY CONFIDENCE REFLECTION

Day 19

Boundaries support my sanity.

DAILY CONFIDENCE REFLECTION

Day 20

All of me wants to win.

DAILY CONFIDENCE REFLECTION

Day 21

The moment I listen to me, the closer I am to freedom.

DAILY CONFIDENCE REFLECTION

Week 4: Counteract Confidence Barriers

"You cannot stumble upon greatness; you walk up to it and introduce yourself."

Christin L Webb

The Owl

When I think about an animal that represents my personality or what I want to embody, it is the owl. Yes, the owl. I have all types of keepsakes for owls. When you visit my home, it is common to see statues, trash cans, dishes, jewelry, pillows, lights, and more designed as or around owls. Owls are known for so many different things. They are known for their distinctive features and behaviors. Often recognized for their large, forward-facing eyes and excellent night vision, which aids in their nocturnal hunting. They have a well-developed sense of hearing, crucial for locating prey in the dark. Their silent flight is enabled by specialized feathers, making them effective and stealthy hunters. Additionally, owls are associated with mystery in various cultures and folklore, symbolizing knowledge, intuition, and connection to the spiritual world. But my reason for embracing the owl is because of its representation of wisdom. Wisdom to me has always indicated that knowledge has been incurred.

At an early age, I either found myself immersed in wanting to learn or wanting to share what I learned. When I do not know the answer to something I find myself profusely seeking out the answer so I can add it to my knowledge bank. The way I look at it, the more I learn, the more effective I am. That effectiveness comes from the wisdom I use with the knowledge I gain. Therefore, I why I embrace owls as what I hope to embody the most- wisdom.

In my last corporate role, the unfamiliar territory forced me to face my confidence head on. The executive role was new for me, and I had much to learn. Outside of the administrative components of learning a job, I also had policy, team dynamics, company culture, politics, and more to learn. Whew. It was a lot. I sometimes felt ill-equipped because I did not always have the answer for certain scenarios when I first began. I lost many thoughts; sometimes even rest, over 'not knowing.' That is what unfamiliar territory looks like though. Having the answer is not a guarantee.

The lack of knowledge was a barrier to my confidence. So, I studied. I took in all the knowledge I could. I learned the policies. I learned the processes. I became more astute about the company culture and the main characters. I interviewed people. I took notes. I researched. I studied meetings and behaviors in meetings. I benchmarked the industry, often. I strategized. I increased my knowledge and competence in the new role.

It took approximately two years once I felt fully competent in the knowledge required for my role. I felt unstoppable following that period. Once I knew what I knew, I knew I knew, my confidence skyrocketed; my performance became more consistent and solid. I had transitioned from embracing the owl to becoming it.

What tools do you use to help manage your confidence?

Step 4: Counteract Confidence Barriers

Increasing confidence in challenging situations can be achieved through identifying and practicing emotional, mental, and physical strategies. By mastering these techniques, it becomes easier to manage previously experienced difficult situations. Understanding how to overcome these barriers enables proactive use of various actions, thoughts, and strategies, reducing the likelihood of these barriers reemerging. To enhance your confidence, identify actions from the provided list that you can start implementing today, tomorrow, in the next month, and beyond. Regularly execute these tasks, monitor the results, and observe the positive changes in your confidence levels.

Emotional
Tapping into and being aware of our emotions can support our ability to counteract low confidence. Recognizing and understanding emotions, such as fear or anxiety, helps in addressing the underlying causes of low confidence. By being emotionally aware, individuals can develop strategies to cope with negative feelings, build resilience, and foster a more positive self-view. This emotional intelligence plays a key role in enhancing self-assurance and confidence.
- Depend on self-first.
- Secure a mentor.
- Get to know yourself.
- Be grateful.
- Embrace, assess, & process your emotions.
- Practice mindfulness.

Mental
Science indicates that our thoughts significantly influence our actions and behavior. This concept, often rooted in cognitive psychology, suggests that the way we think about ourselves, and

our abilities can shape our confidence levels. When we focus on understanding and managing our thought processes about confidence, it enhances our awareness of our own state of confidence. This heightened awareness allows us to recognize areas where we may lack confidence and to take appropriate actions to build it, thereby influencing our behavior in a positive way.

- Ask questions.
- Think positive thoughts.
- Meditate.
- Be organized in thought.
- Focus on solutions.
- Increase competence.

Physical
There are physical actions that can be utilized to activate during times of low confidence. These actions trigger physiological responses that can enhance feelings of confidence and reduce anxiety.

- Practice breathing exercises.
- Journal.
- Verbalize affirmations.
- Practice good hygiene & grooming.
- Practice good articulation
- Be organized.
- Exercise.
- Set & achieve a small goal.
- Volunteer.
- Stand tall.
- Complete a presentation.
- Talk to a stranger.
- Resolve a conflict.
- Smile.

Confidence Barrier Counteractive Strategy

To develop a strategy for overcoming confidence barriers, use the Confidence Barrier Counteractive Strategy and follow this assessment matrix:
- Pinpoint an instance where you experienced low confidence.
- Detail the environment, people, and circumstances contributing to this lack of confidence.
- Apply the listed emotional, mental, and physical methods to identify specific actions that can help you overcome or eliminate the barriers.

Identified Barrier	Description of the Barriers Ecosystem	Counteractive Action

Day 22

I am activated to growth.

DAILY CONFIDENCE REFLECTION

Day 23

My truth is in the discovery.

DAILY CONFIDENCE REFLECTION

Day 24

I am my competition.

DAILY CONFIDENCE REFLECTION

31 Days of Confidence: Engage Your Core and Leadership

Day 25

I remove the spaces that do not serve me.

DAILY CONFIDENCE REFLECTION

Day 26

The person, thing, or circumstance that tried to knock me out will not win.

DAILY CONFIDENCE REFLECTION

Day 27

I have the authority.

DAILY CONFIDENCE REFLECTION

Day 28

I allow my power to become my influence.

DAILY CONFIDENCE REFLECTION

Week 5: Inspire Confidence

"You cannot stumble upon greatness; you walk up to it and introduce yourself."

Christin L Webb

The Legacy of Women's Month

I sat in the back of the church sanctuary on the wooden pew staring at the women of the church who led the services during Women's Month. They were schoolteachers, musicians, choir directors, administrative professionals, mothers, sisters, aunts, community activists, and other varying titles. It was always an inspiring moment for me. When I was younger, it was less likely to see a woman in a leadership role on a regular basis; let alone a more prominent role. Until my later teen years and early twenties, most women I saw played in supporting roles only. Back then I did not realize that even in their supporting roles they were leaders.

Women's Month was one of the few times of the year that I saw women leading service in every capacity. It was one of the first times I ever witnessed a woman minister preach. I was floored. It was unheard of. It was shocking, but I embraced it because she was me. Yes, even at ten and eleven years old, I knew what inspiration felt like and what it meant to feel power from someone else's. I could feel the transfer of energy in her commanding of the room, her sharing a vision, and using her voice to impact hundreds. She stood confidently on the pulpit that Sunday morning. Her stature, while not very tall, was as elevated as the building we all stood in. Her voice was purposeful. She spoke boldly. She spoke with intent. Her voice rose with confidence. She demonstrated who she was unapologetically and authentically. The audience sat on the edge of their seats, hanging on to every word that rolled from her lips. She shared passion and facts. She was confident. When she was done, the audience rose to their feet in applause. By the end of her message, I was her. She became a part of me. I became the confident woman that stood before the congregation. Her power became my power. Her influence became my influence. Her charismatic prowess and articulation helped shape mine. It is so dynamic to know that one person can influence and inspire confidence in someone else. That day I was ready to take on the world.

The minister was not the first or the last person to inspire confidence in my life. The list is too long to continue. There were supervisors, mentors, friends, family, business owners, collegemates, colleagues, community leaders, business acquaintances and more. That inspiration has often come when I least expect or want it sometimes. It is necessary, as we never do it alone. While confidence is important for the leader to be effective, it is no less important for those influenced by the leader. I wonder how many people sat in the church with me that day; in one of the pews and shared the minister's confidence with me. I know I was not alone.

There are many times in life we encounter people that inspire confidence within us. They help us stay motivated, driven, and focused. They help us trust ourselves and the things we bring to the table. Leaders who inspire confidence help strengthen the thread of success for each individual team member, the organization, and the community. How we choose to use that inspiration is something everyone must answer to. Even more so, how we choose to inspire confidence is meeting the call of servant leadership.

Step 5: Inspire Confidence

High confidence levels not only benefit the individual but also positively influence those around them, especially in leadership roles. When leaders display confidence, they become a source of inspiration and learning for their team members. This demonstration of confidence can empower others, fostering their growth and encouraging them to embrace similar confidence in their endeavors.

Shared confidence refers to a collective sense of assurance and capability within a group or team. It is not just about individual members being confident; it is about the group developing a unified confidence in their abilities and goals. This shared belief enhances teamwork, collaboration, and effectiveness, as members support and reinforce each other's confidence, leading to a stronger, more cohesive unit.

Inspiring confidence in others can lead to the development of shared confidence within a group or team. When a leader or individual exhibits confidence, it sets a positive example and creates an environment where others feel encouraged to also display confidence. This shared confidence can enhance the group's overall performance, foster collaboration, and improve decision-making processes. Confidence becomes contagious, empowering each member and strengthening the collective capabilities of the team or organization.

Identify individuals in your life that you can positively impact and help foster high confidence in them.

"Service is the rent we pay for the privilege of living on this earth."
-Shirley Chisholm

B.U.I.L.D. Shared Confidence

To foster sustainable shared confidence in teams and organizations, it is crucial to inspire confidence in others through various strategies. To create shared confidence, consider the strategy of believing, understanding, investing, leveraging, and developing skills that is sustainable.

How can you inspire and build shared confidence?

Believe
- Exhibit your own confidence.
- Have faith in your team's abilities.
- Share a clear vision for the future.

Understand
- Clearly define goals and expectations.
- Value and implement diversity.
- Actively listen.
- Treat everyone with respect.

Invest
- Encourage collective learning.
- Positively reinforce team members.
- Celebrate their achievements and milestones.

Leverage
- Use failures as learning opportunities.
- Provide chances for realignment.
- Lead by example.

Develop
- Support personal and professional growth.
- Offer coaching and mentorship.
- Delegate responsibilities.
- Discuss performance openly.

By implementing these practices, you can build and maintain a culture of shared confidence.

Day 29

I give the energy I want to receive.

DAILY CONFIDENCE REFLECTION

Day 30

My time is precious.

DAILY CONFIDENCE REFLECTION

31 Days of Confidence: Engage Your Core and Leadership

Day 31

Joy is mine.

DAILY CONFIDENCE REFLECTION

The journey of greatness begins with you.

Confidence Post-Assessment
Rate Your Existing Level of Confidence

Congratulations! You have successfully completed **31 Days of Confidence: Engage Your Core and Leadership**! It is important to identify variances in your confidence level from the beginning of the process.

Take a few moments to complete a post-assessment of your existing confidence level. Compare it to your initial assessment. Has anything changed? Can you identify areas of growth?

Questions	Not At All	Rarely	Sometimes	Often	Very Often
In my actions, I often prioritize societal expectations over my personal convictions of what's truly right.					
Navigating new scenarios, I find myself adapting with a sense of ease and confidence.					
My outlook on life is generally upbeat and full of energy.					
Confronted with challenges that seem daunting, I'm inclined to step back rather than engage.					
Persistence is a trait I hold dear, continuing the effort where others might retreat.					
I'm convinced that diligence in problem-solving inevitably leads to uncovering solutions.					

Setting goals for myself, I consistently meet them.					
Encountering difficulties can sometimes leave me feeling defeated and pessimistic.					
I empathize with those who invest immense effort yet find their goals just out of reach.					
The feedback I receive on my endeavors and accomplishments is often affirmative.					
Without early signs of success in my endeavors, my motivation tends to wane.					
When I overcome a challenge, I reflect on the insights gained from the experience.					
I hold a firm belief that dedication and hard work pave the way to achieving my aspirations.					
My circle includes individuals whose skills and achievements I admire and deem successful.					

Source: Adapted from MindTools.com and retrieved from the resource article: How Self-Confident Are You? Improving Self-Confidence by Building Self-Efficacy

TOTAL SCORE: _____

Score Interpretations	
14-32	You might be yearning for a boost in self-assurance! Consider reflecting on your accomplishments. Often, it's easy to dwell on what's missing, overshadowing the appreciation and application of your unique skills and talents.
33-51	You're somewhat on track with acknowledging your capabilities and trusting in what you can do. However, you might be setting the bar too high for yourself, which can hinder you from fully embracing and benefiting from your expertise.
52-70	Outstanding! You excel at extracting lessons from each experience, and you don't let challenges diminish your self-view. Remember, there's always space for personal growth. Continue to cultivate your self-confidence with care.

The most sustainable path to success is to engage your core...

Confidence Goals

This activity is designed for you to reflect on your confident journey over the past 31 days. In this section, you will identify key insights about your confidence and outline any goals that emerged from this reflection. Make sure these goals are S.M.A.R.T. – Specific, Measurable, Attainable, Realistic, and Time-bound – to ensure they effectively contribute to your success.

What have you learned about yourself over the last 31 days?

How has this five-step strategy impacted on your confidence?

Do you have goals relative to confidence that have developed? If so, the next steps include defining the goal in the table below and creating a high-level action plan to support the goal(s).

Complete each as follows:

- Identify the confidence goal.
- Determine the goal's level of priority to your journey of leadership (low, med, high)
- Outline objectives to reach the confidence goal.
- Identify the resources needed to accomplish the goal.
- Identify potential risks to be mitigated.
- Create a deadline to reach the goal.

Goal	Priority	Objectives	Resources & Risks	Deadline

Appendix

Confidence Assessment Scorecard

Based on your answers to the pre- or post-assessment questions, use the corresponding points indicated in the chart below. Your total score is the aggregate of the points from each question. This cumulative score represents an interpretation of your current level of self-confidence.

	Pre-/Post Assessment Scoring					
	Questions	Not At All	Rarely	Sometimes	Often	Very Often
1	In my actions, I often prioritize societal expectations over my personal convictions of what's truly right.	5	4	3	2	1
2	Navigating new scenarios, I find myself adapting with a sense of ease and confidence.	1	2	3	4	5
3	My outlook on life is generally upbeat and full of energy.	1	2	3	4	5
4	Confronted with challenges that seem daunting, I'm inclined to step back rather than engage.	5	4	3	2	1
5	Persistence is a trait I hold dear, continuing the effort where others might retreat.	1	2	3	4	5
6	I'm convinced that diligence in problem-solving inevitably leads to uncovering solutions.	1	2	3	4	5
7	Setting goals for myself, I consistently meet them.	1	2	3	4	5
8	Encountering difficulties can sometimes leave me feeling defeated and pessimistic.	5	4	3	2	1
9	I empathize with those who invest immense effort yet find their goals just out of reach.	5	4	3	2	1
10	The feedback I receive on my endeavors and accomplishments is often affirmative.	1	2	3	4	5
11	Without early signs of success in my endeavors, my motivation tends to wane.	5	4	3	2	1
12	When I overcome a challenge, I reflect on the insights gained from the experience.	1	2	3	4	5
13	I hold a firm belief that dedication and hard work pave the way to achieving my aspirations.	1	2	3	4	5
14	My circle includes individuals whose skills and achievements I admire and deem successful.	1	2	3	4	5

Notes

Notes

Notes

Go be GREAT!

About the Author

Christin Webb, an acclaimed motivational speaker, and CEO of The Greater You Leadership Series, excels in fostering transformational leadership. Her expertise over 20+ years in government and contracting, notably as the Chief Procurement Officer in Tennessee, combines with her role as an instructor and consultant to shape leaders and organizations. Since 2019, she has been impacting audiences globally with her "Leading with Confidence" model and empowering women through the "Women Leaders Walk the Talk" community. Also, an international bestselling author and screenwriter, Christin's creativity amplifies her leadership philosophy. Recognized by Ordinary Magazine and Dale Carnegie, she is a dynamic speaker known for her engagements at prestigious venues like the John F Kennedy Center. Holding an MBA, being a certified procurement professional, and a social worker, Christin, a Memphis native, twin, and mother, embodies her belief: *"You cannot stumble upon greatness; you walk up to it and introduce yourself."*

www.ingramcontent.com/pod-product-compliance
Lightning Source LLC
Chambersburg PA
CBHW060403050426
42449CB00009B/1872